THE PRIDE OF BELONGINGNESS

THROUGH THE LIFE OF SAMBHAJI

SAHIL MATHUR

This book belongs to every Young Indian who takes Pride in India's history, heritage and heroes, and finds contentment in associating with India's values.

I dedicate this Book to

My Parents **Mr.Abhishek Mathur and Mrs.Iti Mathur,** My Real-life Superheroes!

Mrs.Mehak Mathur for always providing me with her valuable inputs.

My friend Ms.**Vanshita Rander,** My constant supporter and guide

Contents

Preface

To ensure the optimum efficacy of a country full of young and energetic youth, inspiration and guidance emerge out as the most important psychological factors. It is not a straining task to find inspiration in the great land of India which has a glorious past and a fortunate destiny to witness many of the greatest men ever born on this Earth. Unfortunately, due to a variety of reasons many of such legends have not been given enough place in texts and contemporary modes of knowledge exchange, that can justify the greatness and sacrifice of such great men.

One of the lost legends is that of Chatrapati Sambhaji Maharaj, Chatrapati Shivaji Maharaj's great son, the second Chatrapati of the Maratha Empire.

It is very disappointing to acknowledge the fact that Sambhaji Maharaj's greatness and his story is unknown to an extremely large population of this country, the motive behind writing this book lies in the fact that it is now a matter of prime importance to make this country aware of the values our ancestors catered, the level of patriotism they were filled with and the pride they took in belonging to their nation and their roots.

It becomes important to learn and read about such Hero because, Sambhaji's life is inspiring, motivating and exceptional.His perspective towards life is a benchmark, that the youth of this country should look upto.

The path to a Bright future carved by a Shinning youth is possible only when we learn from our Glorious past !

The Might Of Sambhaji

The name Sambhaji Raze Bhosle carries with itself the epitome of Pride, courage, sacrifice, intelligence, sincerity, and patriotism of the highest order that planet earth has ever witnessed. Spearing through a life full of challenges and dolor the young boy with shine in his eyes and might in his sword emerged to be one of the most glorious and fearless emperors historians could ever boast.

Being born into the great legacy of Chatrapati Shivaji Maharaj brought great responsibilities and difficulties for the furious boy who later went on to defy all odds and justified Shivaji Maharaj's blood. Every breath that Sambhaji Maharaj took was synchronized with the belief and faith of every Maratha and their idea of *swarjya*.

The valour and bravery of Sambhaji Maharaj are unparalleled by any other rulers that existed in his time or even before. Sambhaji and his close associate Kavi Kalash are still unmatched in the level of wit and intelligence they carried.

This prodigy was not only limited to the power of body but what made him different was the power of the mind, Shivaji's proud son was exemplary at his capacities to apply brains with the excellent capacities of creativity. Sambhaji Maharaj wrote magnificent literature in the fields of politics and divinity that are further discussed.

The Undefeatable force of Chatrapati Sambhaji Maharaj could evolve into such power pertaining to the innovation and the commendable knowledge that the smart ruler applied to take an edge over the powerful Mughals.

The very brief description of the valorous Maratha warrior might excite any reader so as to discover how the little boy Sambhaji went on to become the great Chatrapati Sambhaji Maharaj and sacrificed himself at the mere age of 31 leaving behind stories of courage, sacrifice, grandeur and lessons for us to understand, accept and foster the 'Pride of Belongingness'

CHAPTER ONE

Nurturing the Veracious Patriot

Destiny was never kind to the Marathas; it was their valour and spirit to re-arrange the stars that made them an exceptional race, Sambhaji was no exception. Born to Shivaji Maharaj and Saibai on 14th May 1657 at the glorious Purandar fort, Sambhaji lost her mother at the tender age of two and was brought up by his Grandmother Jijabai, the *aaisaheb* (mother) of Shivaji Maharaj. It is evident that Sambhaji had all the qualities of his father as both of them were brought up and given a similar upbringing by one mother Jijabai. Sambhaji's life made him comfortable with loneliness and solitude considering the fact that he lost his mother at an age when he hardly attained consciousness and his father was busy serving a greater motive, to establish swarajya and confront the Mughal ruler Aurangzeb.

Sambhaji Maharaj had to face the wrath of politics at the young age of 9. The fort of Purandar was besieged by Jai Singh 1 the commander of the Mughal army on 11 June 1665. On acknowledging the loss Marathas would suffer, Shivaji Maharaj decided to enter into a treaty with the Mughals, 'The Treaty of Purandar'. As a clause of this treaty, the 9-year-old Sambhaji was sent to live as a political hostage with Jai Singh 1 in his fort of Amer.

In the twentieth century where 9-year-old kids are still considered to be immature enough and are subjected to the utmost care, love and affection by their parents, Sambhaji was brilliantly fulfilling his responsibilities of the treaty. He also used this as an opportunity to learn about Politics and the Collative Political Relations the Mughals under Aurangzeb used to keep with their allies. All his observations and knowledge helped him disquiet Aurangzeb and his men during his tenure on the throne.

The futile attempt to capture the spirit of a Maratha:

On 12th May 1666, Shivaji Maharaj was called by Aurangzeb to his fort in Agra, Shivaji decided to take his young son along with him. Aurangzeb justifying his image of an ill-mannered ruler insulted Shivaji Maharaj, Sambhaji and the Maratha commanders in the court to which Shivaji responded by a walkout. This act of Shivaji was enough to hurt to the little ego of the mighty emperor, as a result he ordered a house arrest of Shivaji and his army. It becomes important to acknowledge that Sambhaji was just a little 9-year-old boy who was as gallant as his father.

This act of Aurangzeb was successful up to some extent to put Shivaji in a stressful situation, but no problem on the planet was big enough for Shivaji Maharaj and neither was this situation too big for the 9-year-old cub Sambhaji. Shivaji was intelligent enough to maintain a decent and healthy communication with Aurangzeb during the house arrest and play a bluff and pretend that he was falling ill, asking for Aurangzeb's consent to send out boxes of fruits and other items for the needy to which he agreed. Shivaji waited for Aurangzeb's soldiers to grow lethargic and stop checking the boxes, on identifying the right time both

Shivaji and Sambhaji escaped the place by getting into similar boxes. Shivaji's close aid Hiroji Farzand replaced Shivaji on his bed to bluff the soldiers and it was much later that the soldiers realised the intelligence of Shivaji, till then Shivaji successfully reached his kingdom fleeing through the Northern and Eastern parts of India.

All of this smartness and political wisdom was experienced by Sambhaji at a very young age which shaped his personality, mind and capacities to think which helped him to rule as no other king could.

After the Marathas signed the Purandar Treaty, the Marathas and Mughals shared a very sophisticated but a considerable political understanding. While his time with King Jai Singh the little Sambhaji was smart enough to misguide them and provide them with spurious or faulty inputs so that his father could draft his plans of *swarjya* without an intrusion of the Mughals.

Chatrapati Shivaji Maharaj was the living incarnation of God to every Maratha who dreamt of a free country. The respect he received was immense and with par his demeanor, to have him as his father was in itself a great matter of pride for Sambhaji Maharaj.

Considering the rising social unrest in the youth and a growing sense of ignorance towards one's parents in the society, the sincerity and respect Sambhaji had for his father serve as an example, from birth till the death Sambhaji was all praises and proud for his great father and the values he inherited from him.

Although history and folklores mention incidents where Shivaji was unpleased by the conduct and behavior of Sambhaji in his youth and even punished him for that but the latter never lost the respect and dignity for his father irrespective of everything!

Sambhaji was not only a brave and valiant warrior but was also a very sophisticated writer who wrote great literature at the young age of 14. His major works include Budhbhushanam which begins with the praise of his Grand Father (Sahaji Maharaj) and Father (Chatrapati Shivaji Maharaj), to express the honor he felt for the family and race he belonged to. The book further goes on to explore the different aspects of politics and the duties and responsibilities of a good king. He also wrote 3 popular Hindi *Granthas* related to various aspects and disciplines of literature. He was well versed in around 13 languages by the time he turned 13. These languages included Marathi, Hindi, Sanskrit, Braj, Persian etc.

The making of a warrior starts from the very time he learns to think and makes a point of view, Sambhaji was blessed to be brought up by one of the strongest mothers Jijabai and to witness one of the strongest warriors that ever-existed Shivaji Maharaj.

Sambhaji was faced with probably all the difficulties in his childhood that one could imagine, but he never failed to learn from every situation and excel in whatever task he was expected to do.

The youth today is struggling to find help when life confronts them with the hurdles that are eventually meant for their learning, they fail to acknowledge the importance of struggle and challenges in personality making. The story, journey and the entirety of Sambhaji Maharaj's childhood may prove to be an eye-opening realisation for the young India.

CHAPTER TWO

The Impediment

Under the regime of Chhatrapati Shivaji Maharaj, the Maratha Kingdom guarded by the hills of Sahyadri attained new glories. Being the eldest son Sambhaji considered his moral responsibility to uphold and emulsify the prestige his father won for the Marathas, but Destiny was not kind enough to let Sambhaji claim his deserved throne in a tranquil manner.

The growing stature of Shivaji invited resistance from the other ambitious leaders and commanders of the Maratha clan. This envious resistance was identified by the Mughals. The Mughals were known for their manipulation and negotiation skills, they were smart enough to identify the malicious yet influential subjects of Shivaji's court and showered them with promises of power and money if they could help Mughals to capture or even execute Shivaji Maharaj.

All of this was done through very sophisticated and elaborated planning. A step in the plan was to defame and raise concerns over the character of Sambhaji. Vishwas Patil in his book 'Sambhaji' illustrates that it became a periodic practise for the particular grudged group to associate Sambhaji's name with different women garnished with made up stories. All of this was done to question his character and move the subjects in believing that he is not a legitimate and appropriate candidate to claim Shivaji's throne. Although these manipulated insinuations did not strike Sambhaji initially but the gradual repetition for such allegations raised concerns for Shivaji for he was worried about the attempts made to tarnish the image of his successor. Sambhaji was perceptive enough to identify the conspiracies against him and ignore them effectively, what he could not accept was his own father whom his praised like God doubting him. Although in the past a young and docile Sambhaji was involved in an unfortunate happening that instigated as the false base of rumours conspired against Sambhaji. It becomes important to highlight the fact that Shivaji was a man of wisdom and did not believe in vagueness of claims but when the allegations came through his most trusted men, he preferred keeping the King's conduct superior to that of a father.

Sambhaji was fortunate and blessed enough to have an intelligent and strong woman as his better half 'Yesubai'. Yesubai was a young, smart and confident women who always stood at par with Sambhaji and did not allow the tsunami of rumours around to affect her conscience and doubt her husband. Shivaji always believed in the character of his son and was soon joyfully abundant with enough proofs of satisfaction that entirely removed the falsified doubts from his unbiased will.

Sambhaji was not only subjected to defamation and attempts of derogation from the conspirators, rather he had to fight his family to claim the throne that he rightfully deserved. Although Shivaji and Sambhaji shared one of the most respectful and lovable relationship, but it becomes difficult for two extremely powerful people to be on the same page at every matter of opinion. Sambhaji was young and rebellious who had a different approach towards politics and other matters of state. As a result, he did not have a healthy rapport with every member of Shivaji Maharaj's *'ashthpradhan'* his 8 primary and most trusted ministers, moreover Sambhaji was also subjected to extreme dislike by his stepmother Soyarabai. She was under a doubt that Shivaji Maharaj would hand over the entire Maratha Empire to Sambhaji and her 10-year-old son Rajaram would be given nothing.

Soyarabai found support in the ministers who were already against Sambhaji and his ideologies and convinced Shivaji to not take Sambhaji with him in the expedition to win Karnataka. Shivaji had to accept Soyarabai's terms as he was afraid of her threats of starving herself if he did not agree. He was resistant of a tussle in the Royal Family come to public eyes. As a result of her threat, Sambhaji was sent to Shringarpur. While spending his time at Shringarpur Sambhaji still took his responsibility and decided to have an update of activities being conducted in his empire which again led to a series of banters and arguments between him and few of the esteemed commanders and leaders.

After being back from Karnataka, Shivaji was welcomed with complaints and dissatisfaction with Sambhaji's conduct by Soyarabai and a few other courtiers like Annaji Datto. Shivaji was compelled to send a letter to his beloved son, a letter filled with anger, humiliation, and shame. The young Sambhaji was furious at the fact that his father did not even consider calling him to his court and addressing him personally rather choose to send a letter, he was disturbed by the fact that his father lost faith him. Sambhaji's relationship with his father was such that he could have survived all thorns of the worldly plant to get the fragrance of Shivaji's love and company. As a kid he was deprived of the privilege to spend time with any of his parents hence he wanted to be around his father as much he could. It became difficult for a heartbroken Sambhaji to accept this emotional distance being created between him and his father.

Sambhaji then decided to be entirely on his own and accepted an invitation by Dilir Khan a close aid of Aurangzeb and visited his camp where he received a grand welcome and extraordinary gifts. Mughals got a clue about the sourness that emerged in the father-son relationship which made them hungry enough to utilise this opportunity to their benefit. After spending a few days in Dilir Khan's camp, he sensed something suspicious and decided to escape from an unannounced hostage and found residence at the fort of Panhala but the rough patch of life was not over for Sambhaji here.

The year was 1680 and The Lion left his kingdom, Shiromani Chatrapati Shivaji Maharaj was no more. Sambhaji's lord, his idol was no more. The roots of the conspiracy were so deep that Soyarabai managed to let Sambhaji remain unaware of this incident and held him under custody in Panhala. She initiated the rituals to announce Rajaram as the heir of Shivaji. As soon as this information reached Sambhaji he escaped the fort and reached Raigad where he claimed the throne he deserved and was eventually announced as the ruler of the Maratha Empire. It is worth mentioning that this was not the last attempt of conspiracy against Sambhaji, there were many attempts made but none of them proved to bear fruits for the conspirators.

These Experiences implicate how important the value of trust is, Sambhaji had Yesubai, whose trust was rock solid in her husband's character. We see that the father-son indulge in differences of opinion and ideologies numerous times but both of them never lose their faith in each other. Moreover, Sambhaji doesn't fail to showcase his extreme devotion to his motherland. He had an option to settle and compromise with the Mughals and let his father's dream of swaraj go in turmoil. Instead, he realized the blunder he might commit and stuck to the faith and mission of his father proving that he was indeed the blood of Shivaji.

It is evident that Sambhaji took pride in belonging to his father, his wife and his motherland. Irrespective of all the humiliation conspires and challenges Sambhaji's pride reminded him of his duty, to serve the Martha Empire and carry on with his father's dream of Swarajya.

CHAPTER THREE

The Continuance of Legacy

Sambhaji's coronation was the first letter in the golden pages of glorified Maratha history. Soon after Sambhaji took charge the Maratha Empire was on a sortie to win the greatest battles.

History dictates that every powerful ruler with a heart full of courage necessarily requires a company of a mind full of wisdom. Sambhaji found his logician companion in 'Kavi Kalash', an intellectual and smart poet who played an extremely important role in shaping Sambhaji's valour for major matters of state. Kavi Kalash was one of his most loyal and smartest friends who admired Sambhaji on every good decision he took and corrected him on every bad one he was about to take. Sambhaji was as accepting and open-minded as Shivaji. In spite of Cold disapproval from the elites of the empire, Sambhaji had his close men selected entirely based on their merits and personality irrespective of their caste. Sambhaji was young and energetic but his approach as a ruler of the state was way ahead of his age and time.

His potential can be understood through the fact that he forced the mighty and apparently undefeatable

Aurangzeb to shift his place of power and come down to the Deccan and settle at Aurangabad. This marked the fall of the Mughal Empire as it weakened their then firm grip in North India and resulted in losing their control from all over the country.

After Shivaji's sad demise Sambhaji went through a lot of hardships to be rightfully claimed as the next Chatrapati. Any ordinary heir would have eventually taken time to enjoy the merits of the position but Sambhaji was not an ordinary warrior. As soon as he took command, he was quick and responsible enough to admit the weakened tressure of the Marathas due to prolonged wars, Sambhaji's response to this issue was not ordinary either.

Sambhaji's approach was assertive and fearless in every manner. After being assigned to the throne Sambhaji decided to raid and attack the fort of Burhanpur, the most powerful Mughal in Deccan. He attacked and looted Burhanpur, damaging the financial and military capacities of the Mughals. This tarnished the image of the enormous Mughal Empire.

Aurangzeb's cruelty was inclusive to his own family, he claimed the throne by putting his father under arrest and murdering his siblings. In continuation to his obsession with power he never tried to maintain a healthy relationship with his sons leading to jeopardy in his family. 'Akbar' Aurangzeb's fourth son was the first one who decided to rebel against his father and found exile in Sambhaji's territory in anticipation of Money and Men to lead a war against his father. Sambhaji rather chose to help Akbar escape to Persia.

Shivaji's dream of swarajya was a belief that the entire India should be freed of the invaders who disallowed the practice of the values of the land. Invaders emphasised conversion along with damaging the beliefs, sentiments and heritage of the land. Other than Mughals one such opposition were the Siddis. Under Shivaji's rule, Siddis were reduced to a very narrow and limited area which made them enter into an alliance with the Mughals. As a result, the Maratha army personally accompanied by Sambhaji went on to attack the fort of Janjira and destroyed their defence. As mentioned earlier Sambhaji was way ahead of his time and age and hence we observe an excellent utilisation of spies under his regime. He understood the depth and importance of military and administrative intelligence which helped him get rid of traitors and also be pre-aware of the enemy strategies.

Sambhaji identified that Mughals outperformed the Marathas in terms of both arms and army, he concluded that depriving them of arms supplies would be the appropriate and optimal solution. The Portuguese in Goa emerged as a prominent supplier of imported arms and artillery to Aurangzeb's army, Sambhaji launched a series of deadly attacks on the Portuguese and demolished their ports to pieces. The Maratha attack was so lethal that the Portuguese viceroy Francisco de Távora was forced to hide out in a cathedral where Saint Francis Xavier's body was kept. The viceroy asked for deliverance from the saint by keeping his baton and royal credentials in the open casket with the saint's body in it. Although Sambhaji had to withdraw his campaign after the Mughals sent their army and navy to Goa.

The Maratha army was in desperate need of modern ammunition to keep their combat for swarjya alive. Sambhaji addressed the urgency to modernise his army and decided to obtain supplies from the British by entering into various agreements with them.

The Mighty Aurangzeb could not tolerate a young kid smashing his existence in the Deccan, he grew hostile and made every mind in his court only think on how to get rid of Sambhaji. Aurangzeb decided to attack the Maratha empire from all directions at the same time, little did he know that the kid sitting on the throne of the Maratha empire with Shivaji's blood in his body was an exceptional prodigy who was prepared for such invasions well in advance.

Mughal army tried to enter Sambhaji's kingdom for 5 long months with constant attacks from all sides. But Sambhu raja's strategy and execution were perfect up to such an extent that he diluted every attack along with assuring minimal damage to his side. The Mughal army outnumbered the Marathas by many times and still proved to be futile in front of the dauntlessness of the 'Veer Marathas'. The guerrilla war tactic in which the Marathas were maestros under Shivaji's leadership was extensively used by Sambhaji as well.

Shivaji was known for his genius in developing war tactics and customising artilleries and military equipment. Alike his father, Sambhaji was a genius as well, he collected different artisans of the kingdom such as cobblers and tailors and developed resources using their expertise. One such innovation was of developing arrows with rubber cloth wrapped around them so that when fired the rubber cloth doesn't burn out early and sustains the fire in the arrows when shot. Later these arrows were complemented with gun powder which when hit the target caused a blast, damaging the defence of the enemy.

Sambhaji was a prodigy, also he was blessed to be born to a great father who helped him learn, that nothing can be conquered out of only physical or intellectual excellence but an efficient combination of both traits is a must. Sambhaji recognized the importance of making friends, he was a man who could see through the person hence all of his friends were men of character and qualities.

His belief in his men and his commanders were the primary reason for his extremely successful military expeditions. His strategies assisted with the commendable administrative-advice from his advisor Kavi Kalash and other ministers brought new glories to the Hindavi Swarajya under Sambhaji's reign.

The important observation from this chapter lies in the fact that Sambhaji knew the skill to ensure the involvement of each and every being of his kingdom in the mission of attaining swarajya. He knew the importance of igniting the pride of belongingness into the hearts of every Martha.

Today when a 'self-centric' lifestyle is claiming popularity, it is important for us to learn that Teamwork and inclusive participation of every social element are the base pillars of the growth and success of a Nation.

CHAPTER FOUR

The Paradigm of Devotion

The 31-year-old Maratha rattled the mighty Mughals for around 9 years in more than 120 battles and no one could ever defeat the brave Maratha knight.

Under the leadership of Sambhaji, the Maratha empire was able to create a strong plinth on financial fronts. His policies regarding trade and agriculture proved fruitful and gave hope for establishing a good economic network in the territory. He gave a strong message that the downfall of Aurangzeb has begun. This strong retaliation by the Marathas gave time for other Hindu rulers in the north to get their backs straight and prepare a strong opposition for the Mughal rulers. Under Shivaji's rule, the widespread caste-based bigotry was reduced to a large extent and continued to reduce in Sambhaji's rule, strengthening the harmony and social structure.

Indian history shows us accounts where mighty legends were subjected to traitors who knowingly or unknowingly to satisfy selfish means compromised the trust of great men. Unfortunately, Sambhaji's story is also a constituent of historic accounts of heroes who were banked by traitors.

Sambhaji's brother-in-law Ganoji Shirke was the traitor who betrayed him and became the sole reason to stain the history of Marathas with the blood of a most cruel and inhuman torture the world has heard of till date. When Sambhaji refused to give Ganoji 'Watan' which he believed he deserved Ganoji grew hostile and turned a traitor.

Sambhaji and Kavi Kalash were on their way to meet the most trusted 25 commanders of the Maratha army, this was not known to all. Regrettably, Ganoji was one of the very few people who was aware of this. Since, he was already malcontent at Sambhaji, he leaked this information to Aurangzeb who was quick enough to send about a thousand soldiers to capture and abduct Sambhaji Maharaj and Kavi Kalash. Both of them were then taken to the Bahadurgad fort to be presented in front of Aurangzeb.

The sadist Aurangzeb crossed all limits of being inhumane and lost every drop of integrity in his blood. As soon as Sambhaji Maharaj along with Kavi Kalash were brought to Aurangzeb's territory, he ordered to dress them as clowns and parade them in front of the public. He decided to humiliate them in the worst possible manner. Aurangzeb ordered his soldiers and public to spit, urinate, throw stones, assault and mock both of them in any manner they could.

After this inhumane and boorish treatment, Aurangzeb confronted Sambhaji and Kavi Kalash and offered to free them and reward them provided Sambhaji surrendered all his forts, open up with the names of the Mughal collaborators and converted himself to Islam. Aurangzeb had no clue that the man in front of him was a hundred times braver and a thousand times more valiant than what he would have imagined. Sambhaji denied to give even 1 inch of Maratha land to the Mughals and denied the offer to convert his religion. Aurangzeb felt insulted and could not digest the fact that Sambhaji was still not close to accept his defeat.

Aurangzeb's ego was shallow to such great depth that he then decided to torture Sambhaji and Kavi Kalash in a manner no human can imagine. He ordered to pull out their nails and hair followed by inserting red hot rods in their eyes and their tongues were pulled out of their mouths. All this while Aurangzeb kept on asking Sambhaji Maharaj the same 3 questions and Sambhaji never expressed his assent to even a word of whatever he said. It is said that Aurangzeb called Sambhaji to his court and again pressed him to convert to Islam and since Sambhaji's tongue was torn he asked for a pen and paper and wrote that he would not convert to Islam even if the ruler offered him with his daughter's hand. Sambhaji's love and devotion to his religion and his resistance towards the concept of conversion earned him the title of *"Dharamveer"*.

This resistance of Sambhaji left Aurangzeb stupefied and furious at the same time. This incident is said to be followed by Mughal soldiers tearing Sambhji and Kavi Kalash's skin part by part leaving their wounds to bleed. Both of them were left as nothing but a breathing piece of flesh. This torture continued for more than a fortnight, at last when Aurangzeb sunk in with the fact that his cruel and crocked mindset was not fruitful to touch the dedication and grace of the *'Veer Maratha'* he ordered his men to tear Sambhaji and Kavi Kalash's body into tiny pieces using *'wagh nakh'* (tiger claws). Aurangzeb's barbaric psyche persuaded him to step down to the lowest level of dignities while executing Sambhaji and Kavi Kalash.

Different accounts narrate different stories to what was done with the shattered and destructed bodies of Sambhaji. Some accounts claim that the pieces of their bodies were fed to dogs while some say that they were thrown near the river banks of Tulapur where the Marathas gathered the pieces and stitched them together to cremate them with dignity and swore to rise back with a more powerful retaliation to the Mughal armies.

After Sambhaji's execution, the Marathas rose with power and they grew to expand their territories weakening the roots of the Mughal empire. The disrupted Mughal rule and the ongoing power tussle in the country was later utilised by the British as an opportunity to take over the country.

In the 21st century, where people and specifically the youth are attracted towards the glamorous and prosperous life in the west and subside their responsibilities and duties towards their nation, Sambhaji appears as the name and story they need to come across. The 31-year-old young man went through one of the cruelest tortures in the history of mankind to fulfill his duties towards his nation and his *dharma*. He could have easily agreed to Aurangzeb's terms and lived a life of relative comfort but he decided to keep the dignity of his nation and his dharma above all. He was a loyal and obedient son who went through the highest degrees of pain but did not compromise with the dream his father saw.

The torture Shambhu raja went through is unimaginable. His will power, dedication and determination are unparalleled and worth worshiping in today's time. His story is a reflection to every citizen of this country who knowingly or unknowingly considers personal interests above national interests. It would not be a justified expectation to imagine the same level of patriotism and dedication in today's time, but every citizen of this great land must not forget to acknowledge their duties towards this nation, its great history and its great values.

Sambhaji's entire life is a lesson for every living being, who caters an ambition and a goal in his life. He is the appropriate idol for people who believe that everything on the face of this earth can be achieved with sheer dedication.

His acknowledgment of his roots and his value of pride towards every aspect he belonged to; his motherland, his religion and his father ignited an entirely divine level of tolerance, power, and valour in his body, mind and soul. The man taught this world that the basis of every ambition and the root of every pillar of success is laid on the "Pride of Belongingness".

Shivaji Maharaj's son lived like a Tiger whose one move was enough to shake the entire armies of his enemies. He ruled like a Tiger who could go to any limit to protect his family and his people. He also died like a Tiger, his will undefeated by any torture and his heart filled with pride till his last breath.

'देश धरम पर मिटने वाला, शेर शिवा का छावा था।

महा पराक्रमी परम प्रतापी, एक ही शंभू राजा था।।'

(Willing to sacrifice himself for his nation and dharma, Shivaji's son was a Tiger indeed. The courageous the majestic, there could ever only be one like the great Shambhu Raja)

• 20 •